DEATH.

A CHRISTIAN'S DILEMMA

Teresa Railey Sancho

God's blessing
Teresa

Bible Reference:
The Holy Bible, English Standard Version. ESV® Text Edition: 2016. Copyright © 2001 by Crossway Bibles, a publishing ministry of Good News Publishers.

Published in the United States of America:

Teresa Railey Sancho
Independent Publisher
Tallahassee, FL 32317

Email: sanc9755@gmail.com

ISBN: 9798409971960

Cover designer: Coffeebrat2020@gmail.com

Dedication

This book is dedicated to those who grieve.

Special thanks to:

Soror Eva B. Mannings, for encouragement.
Dr. Sally P. Karioth, for manuscript review and assessment.

Table of Contents

INTRODUCTION

Is grief an indication that we are not faithful to God's plan? As Christians, we know the love of Christ and the hope we have in Him. It is through that hope that we face the trials of life, which includes death. If death should come our way through a close loved one (child, parent, spouse, etc.), we expect to be able to deal with it and not grieve as those who do not know Jesus or the hope in Him (I Thessalonians 4:13). Many would probably agree that a Christian should manage death well due to the faith factor—the hope that lies within. But when death comes, especially to one who was so dear, that hope can get lost. Just like a lump sitting heavy on the heart, grief blocks everything except the pain and shock that are so overwhelming.

The death of a close loved one can shatter the very foundation of faith one has in Jesus Christ. This can be even more profound when it is unexpected, and the death of a child can compound it even more. Heart and mind race in all directions to comprehend what has happened while frantically searching for faith we own in Christ. We know it is there, but the reality of the pain is too great. How do we react? If we weep and wail, would we appear as one who has no faith? Is there a specific way one who claims to be a Christian should respond?

Take my journey with me in the pages of this book and learn how a loved ones' death put a spotlight on my Christianity. This was showtime; it was time to walk the talk.

1.

THE TRIAL

Railey DaNetta Sancho, my daughter, died of meningococcal meningitis on Saturday, May 5, 2001. Meningococcal disease is a bacterium that can lead to serious blood infections in the brain and spinal cord linings. The symptoms are similar to the flu or sinus cold infection, such as a general poor feeling, fever, headache, nausea, and body aches, and it is contagious. A reddish or purple skin rash, which could mean a bacterial infection in the bloodstream, needs immediate medical attention. Meningococcal meningitis can be fatal or cause great harm with long-term disabilities such as deafness, brain damage, neurological problems, and even loss of a limb.

May fifth, also known as Cinco de Mayo, is an annual celebration commemorating the anniversary of Mexico's victory over the French Empire at the Battle of Puebla in 1862. It is widely celebrated in America, too. At one time, I liked saying, "Cinco de Mayo" because it sounded like our last name, Sancho. For reasons unknown, I would say it quickly three times. However, over time, in doing so, I found my words changing on the last one to "Sancho's demise." And I would think, "Oh my God, how awful!" I would cringe and wonder how such morbid words could come from that. I would think, "Oh Lord, no." It had been years since I repeated the name of that celebration because I knew how it usually ended. I was not prepared when I finally realized the date Railey died … May fifth, Cinco de Mayo. I was shocked. My heart was even heavier if that was possible, thinking if in any way I could have predicted my child's death, even spoken it into existence. All kinds of thoughts raced through my mind, trying to determine if I could have kept this terrible thing from happening. Was that awful saying a warning message somehow meant to prepare me for this heartbreaking event? It was mind-blowing to know that Railey's demise happened on this date. It is still hauntingly disturbing to think about it.

Friday morning, May 4, 2001, started like most mornings for us in Tallahassee, Florida. Calvin, my husband, and I prepared for work, and Railey got ready for school. However, Railey was much quieter this morning than others. I just assumed she was mulling over the previous evening's track meet. She competed on both her high school's 4x100 and 4x400 meter relay teams at Lincoln High School, and both teams failed to qualify for the Florida High School Athletic Association (FHSAA) Track & Field State Championship. She wanted to make it to state. So, I did not interfere much. I just asked how she felt because her back had also bothered her the night during the track meet. She nodded that she was okay. However, after she had passed, I found out from her friends that she was not feeling okay the entire day. My husband drove her to school. Later, he related that she was quiet and just stared out the window during the ride. Attempting to lighten her mood, he said he told jokes but only received a smile, not her usual laughter. He, too, assumed her mood had something to do with the coming down with a sinus cold as I had a week earlier, for my symptoms were similar. I gave her sinus cold medicine and told her to just rest. Around 9:00 p.m., I checked on her, and she was burning up. I took her temperature, and it was 106 degrees. I was about to panic but then remembered to ask questions to determine her cognizance. I had heard that anyone with a high temperature would be delirious and not respond well. She responded well, so I was somewhat relieved. I put cold compresses on her body and immediately called my health insurance urgent care phone line. I explained the situation to the nurse, and she was convinced that the temperature of 106 had to be incorrect since Railey could respond and was coherent. She asked me to take it again while she waited on the phone. This time it was 102 degrees. I was advised to give her two Advil tablets and call in the morning if her symptoms worsened. By 10:30 p.m., though, Railey seemed to be feeling much better, and the fever had gone. She even talked about eating a little later. My husband and I breathed a sigh of relief that she was getting better and particularly getting an appetite.

That night, my husband decided to sleep in the family room to be close to her room. Around 3:00 a.m., Saturday morning, Railey awakened her dad and said her feet were sore. He picked her up and called out to me as he carried her back to bed. We examined her feet and then her body. We noticed various red spots all over her abdomen and chest area. Immediately, my husband said we were taking her to the emergency room at Tallahassee Memorial Hospital. We had never seen anything like that and knew it needed to be checked out. She did not seem distressed and was quite selective about the clothes to wear to the emergency room. I jokingly told her no one would be there to see how she was dressed.

At first glance, the triage nurse guessed it to be measles. But later, the ER doctor diagnosed it as meningitis. At the time, we were not told the type of meningitis but informed it could be a life-or-death situation. However, the ER doctor thought Railey's chance of survival was good with her being so physically fit. We also learned the spots on her body were leakages of blood that had seeped to the top of her skin, forming the reddish skin rash common to bacterial meningitis. There were plenty of medical staff in and out of Railey's ER room taking blood samples, checking her pain level, administering medicines via IVs; lots of activity. My husband and I took turns leaving the room going to the bathroom praying and pouring our hearts out to God for her. With all of this going on, Railey was calm and kept her eyes on her dad and me. Although she responded yes to medical staff for being in pain, she never exhibited any signs of discomfort. We learned from others who had experienced someone suffering from this illness that they were quite distressed and reacted violently from the pain to the point of being strapped to the bed.

Occasionally, she asked us to rub her feet, which her dad and I were eager to accommodate to make her feel better. She was so calm, which kept us calm and quite hopeful that she would get to go home after a day or two. The Demerol pain medicine soon put her to sleep. Then, the medical staff stated they were moving her to "a more comfortable room." They had us give her a kiss and said they would come to get us as soon as they had her settled.

After a wait that was too long for us, the doctor came back. As he was taking us to her, he stated they had to revive her a couple of times. *Revive her?* Our minds could not absorb what he was saying. We were trying to reconcile in our minds how we saw her last to her needing to be revived. It was not making any sense. The doctor's words were so confusing. We reached a door, and the doctor opened it. It was the Intensive Care Unit (ICU). Our hearts sank! Never, in our minds, did "a more comfortable room" equate to the ICU. Seeing her hooked up in there, we realized something was wrong. My husband rushed out to call family again—this time with urgent, fearful news. He called our minister at Grace Family Fellowship, Jonathan Rakestraw, as well.

The fear became a reality. By 10:00 a.m. on Saturday, May 5, 2001, our beautiful, vibrant, fifteen-year-old daughter had passed away. Railey, our only beloved child, had died of meningococcal meningitis. We were in complete shock. It was unimaginable that a child so well and active the previous day could be gone the next day from symptoms that appeared to be a sinus cold.

Ironically, Railey's exit from this world was just as dramatic and intense as her entrance into it. My expected due date for her birth was April 24, 1986. On the evening of Saturday, April 12, 1986, my husband and I decided to go shopping to look for additional baby items in preparation for the birth of our first child. We had not made it far from home when suddenly, my head started hurting so badly I had to hold it with both hands to try and contain the pain. Of course, that ended our shopping plans. My husband turned around fast and headed back home, though the faster he drove, the worst my headache became. Therefore, he needed to drive slower so that I would not feel any bumps from the car. My headache was just that sensitive and painful. We got home, and I laid down with a cold compress on my head. We did not connect my headache to my pregnancy because I was not experiencing any issues in the abdomen area, and my prenatal appointment earlier in the week had gone well.

Soon, my headache subsided. We did not feel the need to seek any medical attention. I intended to call my obstetrician on Monday to inform him of the weekend's events. However, I never got that opportunity. During the early morning hours of Sunday, April 13, I felt another headache coming on, not as intense as before, but nevertheless, a headache. It felt better when I sat upright in bed, so I dozed back off to sleep in that position. The next thing I knew, my husband was screaming my name, asking me how many fingers he was holding up. I told him that I was not able to focus. Then, I remember him frantically moving about the room and telling someone I needed help.

At some point, things became quiet. I was sitting up in bed, looking around the room, feeling strange as if something was not right but unsure of what. Then two men, who I recognized as paramedics by the way they were dressed, entered our bedroom with my husband. They were all looking perplexed at me. I asked, "What's the matter?"

One of the paramedics replied that something was the matter because I had scared my husband half to death. My husband indicated I'd had some type of convulsion with jerking movements as if having a seizure. A paramedic asked how I was feeling, and I said fine because I was feeling okay. They decided to check me out just to make sure, so I sat on the edge of the bed with my legs hanging off. I was soon asked if I could stand up, and I stated sure because I was quite confident I could do that. As I rose, I fell back on the bed. I stated I had not done that right and attempted to stand again. I fell back again. I saw my legs but could not feel my legs. From that, they determined I must go to the hospital. I had been going in and out of consciousness because I remember events sporadically. After determining I would go to the hospital, I do not remember being transported from our bedroom or apartment.

My husband shared that many of our neighbors were outside watching as I was loaded into the ambulance. I do not remember the ride in the ambulance. I only remember being awakened by my doctor, who met the paramedics at the hospital, telling me that I was about to have a stroke, and they needed to get the baby out by C-section so I could be medicated. I had a toxemia attack.

Immediately after that, a gas mask was placed over my face. I remember thinking I would be asked to count backward. That never happened; I was sedated rather quickly. My husband indicated he was unprepared to welcome our baby daughter being brought out to him immediately after the emergency cesarean surgery because he was not given any news on my condition. This new dad was overwhelmed and fearful. He wondered if he would be raising her alone, and he felt alone, too, because no family members had made it to Tallahassee yet. I was in ICU for a couple of days and was unaware of anything. Glory to God, though, all turned out well. So, as it was that family members had to rush to town due to complications surrounding Railey's birth, they also had to rush to Tallahassee as well at the news of her illness that ultimately ended in her death. On that day, part of my heart broke off and left this earth.

2.

THE DILEMMA

Christ does not let us handle trials alone, but in situations like this, all we feel is alone. And although there are people all around us, even our spouse, we feel isolated in our deep sadness as though we are in a dark, locked box.

On that fateful day in May, my faith was reduced to the proverbial size of a mustard seed. More than ever, I wanted the parable, where God said faith the size of a mustard seed was sufficient, in Matthew 17:20, to be true. I felt I was barely holding on by faith, just that size, if at all.

Later that afternoon, when we got home from the hospital with several family members and friends comforting and grieving with us (with more arriving as the news traveled), I put on Donnie McClurkin's *Live in London and More* CD. Listening to gospel music has always given me strength and hope. I needed that solace and background noise to drown out all the thoughts running through my mind. I was feeling nothing, then feeling everything, and just overall feeling completely lost. I then heard the song "I Will Trust You" that I had been inspired to play repeatedly on the Tuesday earlier in the week before Railey's death. I was listening to music while preparing for work. In the song's introduction, God asked several questions of the believer. One was, "If you lose someone very close to you, would you still trust Me?" Each time I answered yes but said I did not want to think about a loss like that. Well, the instant I heard that song, there was this incredible moment where I thought, "Oh my God, You asked me. You asked me about this, and I said I would trust you. Oh my God!" Then I said, "Okay, Lord, I'm going to have to trust You because I said I would."

Now I felt guilty for grieving because the Lord and I had discussed this death situation, and I had said I would trust Him. I was confused, and I was in a dilemma. Was I trusting God even though I was grieving? Could the two exist together? I supposed this was my dilemma as a Christian, trusting God though experiencing great grief.

3.

THE GUILT

Several months after Railey's death, I often told people I would not ask God why our daughter had to die. We were not immune from death any more than anyone else. In my mind, asking the question would be questioning God's judgment on the matter. I reasoned that knowing the answer would not bring my daughter back therefore, I did not need to ask; but how I wanted an answer. I tried my Christian best not to ask God why this had happened. Well, I failed.

One Saturday morning, home alone and still in bed, I looked toward Railey's room. In past times, I would see her pass by, moving about the house. I wanted to see her pass by. I knew it was not going to happen. I would never see her there again, and the realization of that sent me into a rage of uncontrollable crying. I screamed, "Why, God, why? Why did this have to happen? Why did Railey have to die? I want Railey! I want Railey!" God, I hurt. It felt as if my insides would burst out of my skin.

And there, I had asked the question, why? I did not feel any better after asking it, and I did not get an answer, either. In addition to the pain of missing our daughter, I lay in bed crying now because I felt guilty. I felt unworthy of God's attention. I had questioned my Maker. I should have known better because I knew God. But God is so loving and merciful. His Son dwelt among us (John 1:14) and knows what we go through (Hebrews 4:15). He helped me through my feelings. Without delay, through His Holy Spirit, He led me to understand it was okay to grieve for our baby girl. It was such a comforting feeling that came over me as if He were holding me and rocking me. He knew my frailty and susceptibility, and He knew my pain.

He always knows what we need and exactly when we need it. Shortly after experiencing that, several people called to check on my husband and me, to encourage and remind us that they were praying for us. Prayers helped.

4.

THE PROCESS

I called on the name of Jesus Christ and God continually for strength. I needed Scriptures for assurance. I needed to know Railey knew how much we loved and missed her. I needed to know she was aware of this – even in death. In speaking with our pastors, I wanted them to recite this magic Scripture that would make it all better and put everything in perspective. Our pastors helped as much as possible, but there was no magic Scripture. I felt there had to be one, for God would not let me hurt like this. I had to search for that magic Scripture myself. But in my initial attempts, I found out I could not even lift the Bible. The Bible felt as if it weighed a ton. I truly could not lift it. I was frustrated and felt guilty as I did not understand. I loved God, and I knew this without a doubt, but I was unable to lift my source of strength – His Word.

After several attempts, I cannot recall the number of days that transpired when I could finally lift it. However, when I opened it, I could not read it. Each time I found a verse and began to read, my eyes welled up with tears, and the words were out of focus. All I could do was lay the open Bible against my heart, rock, and cry for help. It was humiliating. Soon, with Christ's strength, I could focus on words and search the Scriptures. I was relieved to finally be able to read His Word. I knew I loved God and still trusted in Him, but there were other things I could not do.

I could not sing songs of praise. When we returned to church, it was difficult for me to sing during service. It was as if my lips had been injected with Novocain. I could not move my mouth to say the words in the songs. I was struggling with believing in the words of the songs. Here, again, I felt guilty because I could not sing. I was professing to be a Christian, and I could not sing praises to the Lord, my Helper. My constant prayer, though, was, "God, please, hold us up and keep us close because You know we're hurting so badly."

5.

GRIEF AMONG SPOUSES

Many people said, "Make sure you and your husband stay close to one another and help each other." There are statistics that state as much as 80 percent of marriages fail after the death of a child. I truly understand how that could happen, considering both of us were so bottled up with pain and grief that talking about it was hard.

I felt numb, and I expect my husband did as well. We were both drowning in our own worlds and our own grief even though experiencing this trauma together. Even with the same reason for grief, one can feel so alone. Grieving did create some distance between us because there were noticeable silent moments. There was not enough talk about how each other was feeling about what happened early in the grieving period because it simply caused pain. We were supposed to know how each other felt. I was busy searching through my memories, trying to figure out if I failed in any way as a parent. I went over and over in my mind on what could I have done differently that would have prevented such a terrible outcome. My "what ifs" were endless. Most times I felt I was sparing my husband from more grief by not bringing up the loss of our daughter even though that was constantly on our minds. Yet, talking and listening to one another is what is needed most.

It is logical that a lack of communication can cause people to drift apart, and I was aware of that possibility. I constantly prayed to God for words to share and conversation to uplift.

What I've learned is, in grieving, one of the keys to keeping the relationship strong is to talk to one another about how each is feeling, without condemnation. Communication is one of the main keys. Listen and pay attention to one another and find out what is comfortable to talk about and some of the limitations of what is not ready to be discussed. Both are grieving from the same experience and, as indicated earlier, more than likely in different ways, so the needs of both will be different. It is necessary to remember that just as one spouse wants to be comforted and held, the other may also want that. It may be easier for one to exhibit that behavior more than the other. Prayer is needed for Christ's strength to be cognizant of the other and react with understanding. That was a hard thing to see and do when we were immersed in our own grief.

Though both spouses are grieving the same loss, each one grieves differently. What memory may overwhelm one spouse may not affect the other the same way. One of the hardest things to do when grieving is to support the other spouse in his (her) grief. Because both have been hurt by the same event, it is easy to assume or say, "Well, he knows what I am going through, so it should be easier for him to help me." It is true that he knew what I was going through, but he was also absorbed in pain. Both are hurting and just want to do nothing except have a moment when it does not hurt. It takes a willing heart, prayer, and the strength of

Christ to put one's self and feelings aside and reach out and comfort the other. That can be extremely hard if one spouse is not receptive to the other's comfort.

Grief manifests itself in diverse ways, and there is a difference between the spouse who has learned to live with grief, as opposed to the one who is living the grief. The one who has learned to live with the grief may appear to have moved beyond where the other is. In a sense, that is true, however, the sting of grief is ever-present.

With my husband and me, my grieving was more internal. Few people knew how heavy my heart was or when I was feeling down. My demeanor gave the appearance that I was managing my grief quite well. By the faith of Jesus Christ and His joy, I was, but the pain was constant. The day Railey died, I remember lying in bed that night thinking of the Scripture: "Weeping may tarry for the night, but joy comes in the morning" (Psalm 30:5). I thought, "I cannot believe I will ever feel joy again." Of course, there was no feeling of joy the next morning; at least not what I had in mind. But I came to understand the joy that God provides through the knowledge of Him and His plan of salvation for humanity. Though suffering, being a recipient of His mercy generated gratitude.

My husband, on the other hand, wore his grief externally. I saw it in his walk, his posture, heard it in his voice, and saw it all over his face. At times, it was almost unbearable to watch. Any type of issue for him was magnified because of his pain. He appeared to be angry a lot, sometimes at me, even at God to a certain degree, I believed. I knew that was his pain. He loved God. This was the man who asked me, after two weeks of dating, "Who is the most important person in your life?"

I thought, "Really, you think it's like that now?" To let him clarify, I answered, "What do you mean?"

He replied, "God should be number one in your life." So as much as he was hurting, I knew he was still depending on God.

Within the first two years of Railey's death, my husband's level of grief was so high I had prepared myself to expect a call from the hospital any day informing me that he was there and had died of heart failure. Railey's death almost drained the life out of him. I believed he felt I did not try hard enough to help him through his grieving, but I felt inadequate. There were times when I tried to comfort with words that were only met with negative responses. Then there were times when I would just let him talk his feelings out and not say anything in return. Well, that was the wrong response, too. There was no right response, no matter what I said or did. I could not do what he wanted most: to have Railey back. He was profoundly sad.

When I saw him, it tended to make me feel sad, even if my day was manageable. I did not want to feel down like that anymore. I was getting better at dealing with the pain. I did not want to regress to his level of grief. I felt deeply sorry for him because I knew he was hurting badly. He was, however, a great comfort to me. I think that was because I was more receptive to it. I knew he was there for me, but I also knew it was only God who could help heal my pain. I realized it was going to take that for him as well, and no matter what I said or did not say, or did or did not do, it was going to take God to help him through this. I loved him and knew he loved me. I prayed for God to give him the peace that only He could provide to quiet his spirit, and at the same time, give me the strength to be there for him.

Learning to live with grief and through grief is a prime example of "letting go and letting God." We must have trust that God will help us handle it. God is faithful (Hebrews 10:22-23).

6.

WALK OF FAITH

Many people have told my husband and me that we have been an inspiration to them in how we handled Railey's death. People often said, "I do not think I could do it." As a matter of fact, my husband had commented on previous occasions, when hearing news about the death of a child, that he would probably go crazy if something happened to Railey. To be honest, I tried to let my mind drift off the edge into a twilight zone. But I can truly testify that our survival has been and is by the grace of God and through the strength of our Lord and Savior, Jesus Christ. For so many days, I wanted to give up. I wanted a time when I did not hurt anymore. I was tired of ruminating about Railey being gone and never coming back. I could not bear ever being able to hold her, kiss her, or talk with her again. I knew I could probably die of a broken heart; I was certain that was going to be my husband's fate. But I also continually prayed to God to keep us close and hold us up, and that He did.

One of our family's ministers called us a few days after Railey died. Unfortunately, in my state of mind at that time I do not recall his name or the specific family member he referenced. He offered encouragement and several times asked me to remember, "God is in control." Throughout the conversation, he asked me, "Now, what are you supposed to remember?" Each time, I never did remember. He would remind me again to remember, "God is in control."

Well, two weeks had passed since the funeral, and I had returned to work. One afternoon, while at work, I became incredibly sad, and I left the building to take a walk and talk to God. I told Him, "I am feeling extremely low, and I do not want to feel better. My daughter is dead. I am hurting, and I want to hurt because she is dead."

I loved her, and I missed her so much. I told Him, "You told us to love and take care of her, and that is what we did. Now she is gone, and I am hurting so much that there are no words to even describe the pain." I wanted to be in a state of nothingness. I told Him, "If You want me to feel better, You better perform a miracle because I feel I am going down to a dark place and do not know if I can come back up." Almost instantly, it seemed as if I was not walking anymore. I was still, and it was as if I was watching a big-screen television. God took me to a time back in 1990 when my husband and I were returning to Tallahassee from Houston, Texas, in two separate cars. He drove his mother's car and trailing behind him I drove our car. We were traveling on I-10, approaching Baton Rouge, Louisiana, and it started to rain lightly. Suddenly, I felt the steering wheel jerk in my hands, and the car hydroplaned off the highway down an embankment (about seven feet, I learned). The car was sliding continuously through the brush in the swamps of Louisiana. I was clutching the steering wheel, hiding my face with my arm, anticipating objects crashing through the window. The car came to a stop, and there was complete silence. I shook my body to feel for any pain because I could not believe it was over, and I was not hurt. I was surprised the door opened so easily. I jumped out of the car and ran up the hill to the highway.

My husband had backed up on the highway to the spot where the driver of an 18-wheeler had stopped. The driver was traveling behind me and witnessed where I went off the highway. As I surfaced, the driver was in total disbelief when he realized I had survived that horrific event he saw. My husband and I just stood there, embraced on I-10, thanking God for His mercies and blessings. I was not injured. When the car was pulled from the swamp, it looked in perfect condition. There were not even any scratches on the paint of the vehicle. When checked by the wrecker mechanic, it only needed a front-end alignment. My husband was able to drive the car to Tallahassee with no problems. God told me, "I was there."

Then, He took me to the time when Mike Smith, a friend of ours, had suffered a terrible life-threatening experience when his appendix ruptured. Because of this, when he was hospitalized, his diagnosis was not good, and we were afraid he would not make it. But he completely recovered. God told me again, "I was there."

Next, He took me to Railey's hospital room. He said, "I was there, too."

It was as if a veil had been lifted off of my mind, and I said, "Yes, Lord, you were there."

Immediately, the words of the minister rang into my mind, "God is in control." God went on to say that He was there at all those events, and He allowed certain things to happen.

He said, "I allowed Railey to die. I did not turn my back, and it happened. I allowed it. I am in control." That is when I understood what "God is in control" meant, and somehow, that revelation just relieved me.

I suppose some might say that should have made me mad at God—that He allowed Railey to die, but it did not. It just made me grasp the greatness and power of God. I remember thinking, "Wow! He is in control of everything, and if Railey were supposed to have survived, she would have." God is just that Great. Nothing slips past Him. This also relieved my guilt feelings that there was something I overlooked and should have done that could have saved her. I understood then that it was not about me but God's purpose for each of our lives. He had a purpose for Railey's short life, and He has a purpose for mine. At the end of that experience, I did not recollect walking all around the building, but I found myself back at the entrance of it. I felt so much better. A miracle had positively taken place. At last, I was at peace with Railey's death.

7.

LEARNING TO LIVE AGAIN

Although I am at peace with Railey's death, that does not mean I have stopped grieving. No, I continue to hurt and miss our daughter passionately. Not many hours pass in a day that I do not think of her. She was part of my being, an extension of me. A part of my heart left this earth when she died. I will continue to miss her for the rest of my life. I cry about her, but I do not cry with hopelessness and despair. I cry because I miss her presence in our lives. I miss the things she would be doing now or would have done, such as high school graduation, college, marriage, etc. God helps me understand that it is okay to live again and be an active part of life. His plan for my life is not done yet.

People have said to me, "Well, at least you have her memories." That is true, but the memories often make me miss her even more. Just because I am a Christian and love God does not mean I will wake up one day and not feel sad or that I will wake up one day and no longer miss my daughter. That makes me no less of a Christian and does not minimize my love of God. What I hope to do is wake up each day and realize that God is with me, and I have the assurance of Christ's strength to make the journey. I depend on this daily.

Occasionally, when I dwell on the fact that Railey is not here, grief overcomes me. But without fail, God always intervenes and quiets my spirit.

8.

THE LOVE OF GOD

I hope that sharing my experiences will help alleviate any guilt that may be felt by a Christian's grief at the loss of a loved one. We are indeed human. We do not become super-human because we know the Lord. It is okay to feel the hurt, pain, and anger when a loved one dies. These emotions are the backbone of grief. The hurt and pain are real, painfully real. Exhibiting that hurt and pain makes us no less a Christian or distances us from God. He knows our fragile hearts. He knows our humanness. After all, He created us. He loves us and is there every step of the way. He taught us how to love because "...He first loved us." (I John 4:19).

Remember, Jesus was moved and showed his sadness at the death of Lazarus. Scripture records, "Jesus wept." (John 11:35). He reminds us in the book of Revelation that the time is coming when there will be no more crying or pain (Revelation 21:4).

With my wounded heart, I cannot even begin to imagine no more pain, but I am certainly looking forward to it. God gave us the strength of His Son, Jesus Christ, to rely on. In Philippians 4:13, we read that we can do all things through Him who strengthens us.

At my weakest moments, the strength of Jesus Christ helps me through. I can truly relate now to the poem "Footprints in the Sand." The author dreamed he was walking along the beach with Christ and saw scenes of his life across the sky. Often, he saw two sets of footprints in the sand, but there were times when there was only one set of footprints. He related that those times where there was only one set of footprints were low points in his life when he suffered anguish and sorrow. He determined, at those times, Christ carried him until he could walk on his own again. I am fully convinced that Christ carried my husband and me during the low periods until we had the strength to walk on our own again. He held us up and kept us close as I had prayed. Praise the Lord!

IN CONCLUSION

It has been over twenty years since Railey died, and the pain of missing her is still ever-present. But it is a different kind of pain. It is an acknowledged pain. An "It is in God's hands" pain. It is less acute and more reconciled. Many people said to us that time would help us heal. To me, to hear that initially was quite insensitive, as if my current heartache was being dismissed. But time did help. It helped us get in control of our emotions.

We are no longer on the verge of tears every minute of the day, and grieving has become more private. Understand me, it does not mean that the hurt is not there anymore. Tears are not as frequent as before, but they never go away. The pain of missing Railey is constant. Not a day passes that she is not on my mind. She was real, and my love for her was real. With God's help, I learned to live with it and became functional again.

I can relate a little to a recovering alcoholic who does not lose the desire to drink but learns to control it. The pain of missing a loved one is always there, but we learn to control the pain rather than the pain controlling us. For me, the strength of Christ was essential to my healing.

I do not feel guilty for my sadness about Railey or "having my moments." Those are God-given emotions. Jesus expressed how He felt about the death of Lazarus. It is okay to grieve, but rely on the help of God and Jesus Christ.

As I Corinthians 10:13 speaks to God's faithfulness, He will always provide a way out of whatever troubles us. I usually get an encouraging word from someone, hear an uplifting song, or a Scripture may come to mind – God provides. Thank You, Lord.

Two years after Railey's death, we had a son, Rajauhn. We are thankful to God for him. He is a true joy in our lives. I know he is a gift from God for both of us. However, I believe more so for my husband to soothe his broken heart, not to mend it, but to soothe it. I am sad Rajauhn will not know his sister personally, though he has seen videos of her. When Railey was 9 years old we started making recordings of the various activities and adventures she was involved in. After her death I gathered all these videos and created one memorial video of her from the age of 9 to 15. I gave copies to some of her cousins and closest friends. Rajauhn had watched this memorial video with me from the age of 2 several times, but it was not until the age of 6 that he realized she was a real person and had lived in *his* home. He noticed the furniture and other things throughout the house in her videos. He was very angry that she was no longer alive and wanted to know why she had to die. He wanted to know what we did with her clothes and other things. He asked many questions, trying to understand why his sister was not here. My heart ached for him. He was growing up and learning the realities of life. I always answered him straight though in a language at his level of understanding. One day on a drive home he asked me one question that caused me to silently scream out to God for help. He wanted to know when we saw her again would she be living with us in our home. I told him that I did not know exactly how all of that would work but that we would see her again. He started crying uncontrollably; I was driving so could not grab him to hold him. I was so distraught and just started singing loudly and sang as many gospel songs as I could remember. He soon calmed down. I talked to him some more then told him that God will help him through this because there are some things we do not know. I was mentally and physically exhausted by the time we reached home. Later that evening, I called on some of my prayer warriors and asked them to pray for God to help Rajauhn deal with the knowledge of the death of his sister and missing her. Over time Rajauhn developed a relationship with Jesus Christ and at the age of 14 decided to be baptized. My husband and I were so happy that he had come to understand the need for Christ in his life and how to demonstrate his commitment to that relationship. I am ecstatic he knows and trusts God.

Romans 8:35 states, "Who shall separate us from the love of Christ? Shall tribulation, or distress, or persecution, or famine, or nakedness, or danger, or sword?" Nothing can, as stated in verses 38-39, "For I am sure that neither death nor life, nor angels, nor rulers, nor things present, nor things to come, nor powers, nor height, nor depth, nor anything else in all creation, will be able to separate us from the love of God in Christ Jesus our Lord."

ABOUT THE AUTHOR

Teresa Railey Sancho is 61 years old and has worked for the Florida Department of Education in Tallahassee, Florida, for over 30 years. She has been married 38 years to her college sweetheart Calvin L. Sancho, owner of RDS Drywall & Acoustics, LLC. She is a proud mother of son, Rajauhn Ducati, a student at Jacksonville University and daughter, Railey DaNetta (deceased and the basis of this book).

Although born in Durham, North Carolina, she was raised in Albany, Georgia, by her mother Willie Bell Railey, along with seven siblings. She attended Clark College (now Clark Atlanta University) in Atlanta, Georgia, where she received a Bachelor of Arts degree in Sociology and, as well, became a member of Alpha Kappa Alpha Sorority, Inc, Alpha Pi Chapter. Her college writings were well-regarded by her college professor, Gretchen Maclachlan, who encouraged her to consider being an author. Being an author was a lifelong dream and has finally been achieved.

Notes

Made in the USA
Columbia, SC
05 March 2022